BOOK OF MATCHES

Simon Armitage was born in West Yorkshire in 1963. In 1992 he was winner of one of the first Forward Prizes, and a year later was the *Sunday Times* Young Writer of the Year. He works as a freelance writer, broadcaster and playwright, and has written extensively for radio and television. Previous titles include *Kid, Book of Matches, The Dead Sea Poems, CloudCuckooLand, Killing Time, The Universal Home Doctor, Homer's Odyssey, Tyrannosaurus Rex versus The Corduroy Kid* and *Sir Gawain and the Green Knight*.

SIMON ARMITAGE
Book of Matches

faber and faber

First published in 1993
by Faber and Faber Limited
3 Queen Square London WC1N 3AU
Reset 2001
Phototypeset by Wilmaset Ltd, Wirral
Printed in Great Britain by TJ International Ltd, Padstow, Cornwall

© Simon Armitage, 1993

The right of Simon Armitage to be identified as the author
of this work has been asserted in accordance with Section 77
of the Copyright, Designs and Patents Act 1988.

A CIP record for this book
is available from the British Library

ISBN 978-0-571-16982-5

8 10 9 7

Acknowledgements are due to the magazines, newspapers, periodicals, journals and anthologies in which some of these poems first appeared; to the organizations and societies through which they were commissioned, and to the companies and corporations responsible for their broadcast or transmission.

Contents

I – BOOK OF MATCHES

'My party piece'   3
'Strike two. My mind works'   4
'I rate myself as a happy, contented person'   5
'I like vivid, true-to-life love scenes'   6
'I am able to keep my mind steadily'   7
'Thunder and lightning hardly ever upset me'   8
'People talk nonsense and I put them straight'   9
'People never push me into doing things'   10
'Mother, any distance greater than a single span'   11
'My father thought it bloody queer'   12
'I am very bothered when I think'   13
'A safe rule in life is: trust nobody'   14
'Mice and snakes don't give me the shivers'   15
'I live in fear of letting people down'   16
'I'm dreaming of that work, *Man Seated Reading*'   17
'Brung up with swine, I was'   18
'Those bastards in their mansion   19
'There are those who manage their private affairs'   20
'æŋkɪˈləʊzɪŋ spɒndɪˈlaɪtɪs'   21
'Let this matchstick be a brief biography'   22
'I've made out a will; I'm leaving myself'   23
'I thought I'd write my own obituary. Instead'   24
'Life'   25
'I have dreams like nightmares where I am deserted'   26
'I think about the time'   27
'I feel I am at the end of my tether'   28
'No convictions – that's my one major fault'   29
'The story changes every time'   30

'Thinking back, they either pulled me like a tooth'   31
'Some unimportant word or phrase'   32

II — BECOMING OF AGE

Map Reference   35
The Lost Letter of the Late Jud Fry   36
To Poverty   38
Tale   40
Reverse Charge   41
You   42
Parable of the Dead Donkey   43
Hitcher   46
Act of Union   47
Cataract Operation   48
On the Trail of the Old Ways   49
Penelope   50
To His Lost Lover   51
Becoming of Age   55

III — READING THE BANNS

'Above me, at the abbey'   59
'At closer inspection'   60
'Tread carefully'   61
'This time the cat'   62
'A dream, a nightmare'   63
'This 1950 Rolls-Royce Silver Wraith'   64
'With her labrador, at night'   65
'Around the cuffs and neck at least'   66
'Nine morning suits'   67
'At this stage in the day'   68
'Your wedding day requires'   69
'Let me put it this way'   70

I — BOOK OF MATCHES

My party piece:
I strike, then from the moment when the matchstick
conjures up its light, to when the brightness moves
beyond its means, and dies, I say the story
of my life –

dates and places, torches I carried,
a cast of names and faces, those
who showed me love, or came close,
the changes I made, the lessons I learnt –

then somehow still find time to stall and blush
before I'm bitten by the flame, and burnt.

A warning, though, to anyone nursing
an ounce of sadness, anyone alone:
don't try this on your own; it's dangerous,
madness.

★

Strike two. My mind works
quickly and well these days,
and I like the look of myself of late:

a little more meat
around the face, a little more bite
at the back of the lungs,
a little more point to the tip of the tongue –
no wonder I've been smiling
like a melon with a slice missing.

At twenty-eight
I'm not doing great,
but considering I came from the River Colne
and its long, lifeless mud,
I'm doing good.

★

I rate myself as a happy, contented person,
in spite of troubles here and there.
Selfish, some have said, but in the main
I take a centre line
and let my fringe flop where the wind blows,
northside or south.

If I move my mouth it's mostly to smile,
or something similar,
and I should run a mile
before making trouble. Truly, it's how I am,
that way, and not one angstrom the other.

Lastly, it has helped me more than I could measure
to separate life into two divisions,
of things that is, and things that isn't.

★

I like vivid, true-to-life love scenes
in a movie. No, that's a lie,
that's when I like love least;
it's the turn of a head or a pale blue eye
that moves me.

Keep love in the mind
and out of the blood, beds
are for sleep, for dreams, for good.

I can see what it takes
to keep a friendship in the heart,
the chest. That's
when I like love best – not locked away
but left unsung, unsaid.
And then the rest.

★

I am able to keep my mind steadily
on one job or plan as long as necessary.
Take, as an example, skimming.
Choose the right stone: not so much circular
but one that sits in that natural spanner
between thumb and trigger finger.
A pocket watch would be too perfect.

Pull!
Keep low. Follow through but leave the trailing arm
and lend that stone a certain r.p.m. of spin

so it kicks, sits up at the taste of water.
Count the fourth, fifth, sixth, whatever else
is extra. Walk home. Drop down
into a wider world.

★

Thunder and lightning hardly ever upset me;
not now, not then, like from school when I took
the longer, lonelier way back through the woods
in those startling, bottle-green afternoons.

And once, at the house of the parish spinsters,
I spied for an hour through the rain on their windows
as one worked a brush through the other's hair,
then raised both arms, surrendered, as the other
lifted her cotton blouse over her, from her, this way
then another, as they came together and fell
below the horizon of the windowsill.

Like water, to carry not to spill,
I went with it, out of the rain, the woods,
the instance of that new, unlikely love.

★

People talk nonsense and I put them straight.
Call me brassneck, call me hard-faced
but in this town the people prefer to be steered,
railwayed, run out for the day
to the beach with a bat and ball, then back again.

Look there, the hourglass or the waistline
of a cooling-tower, or here, the pylons number off
across the heath at arm's length,
or take the strain, holding the line. See
from the observation car the world

my way, put that in your pipe
and light it. People talk nonsense
so I put them straight, and I carry no passengers, just
hard freight.

★

People never push me into doing things
I don't want to do. So I go like a railway guard:
snug in the last of a line of carriages,
left to myself and my own devices.

Sometimes, something might draw my attention:
a goods train bound in the other direction,
the unreadable name of an unmanned station, and sometimes,
if forced, I'll be pressed into action;
to sign for a parcel, or take on diesel.

I shall never be one for the clipping of tickets,
or the checking of toilets, or the passing of comments.
I shall sit, to see from here the signals
changing, to say nothing
of the parallel lines converging, and fading.

★

Mother, any distance greater than a single span
requires a second pair of hands.
You come to help me measure windows, pelmets, doors,
the acres of the walls, the prairies of the floors.

You at the zero-end, me with the spool of tape, recording
length, reporting metres, centimetres back to base, then leaving
up the stairs, the line still feeding out, unreeling
years between us. Anchor. Kite.

I space-walk through the empty bedrooms, climb
the ladder to the loft, to breaking point, where something
has to give;
two floors below your fingertips still pinch
the last one-hundredth of an inch ... I reach
towards a hatch that opens on an endless sky
to fall or fly.

★

My father thought it bloody queer,
the day I rolled home with a ring of silver in my ear
half hidden by a mop of hair. 'You've lost your head.
If that's how easily you're led
you should've had it through your nose instead.'

And even then I hadn't had the nerve to numb
the lobe with ice, then drive a needle through the skin,
then wear a safety-pin. It took a jeweller's gun
to pierce the flesh, and then a friend
to thread a sleeper in, and where it slept
the hole became a sore, became a wound, and wept.

At twenty-nine, it comes as no surprise to hear
my own voice breaking like a tear, released like water,
cried from way back in the spiral of the ear. *If I were you,
I'd take it out and leave it out next year.*

★

I am very bothered when I think
of the bad things I have done in my life.
Not least that time in the chemistry lab
when I held a pair of scissors by the blades
and played the handles
in the naked lilac flame of the Bunsen burner;
then called your name, and handed them over.

O the unrivalled stench of branded skin
as you slipped your thumb and middle finger in,
then couldn't shake off the two burning rings. Marked,
the doctor said, for eternity.

Don't believe me, please, if I say
that was just my butterfingered way, at thirteen,
of asking you if you would marry me.

★

A safe rule in life is: trust nobody.
That's the first, and secondly,
the man with 20/20 vision who achieves the peak
of Everest (forgetting for now the curve
of the Earth), looks east and west and gets
a perfect view of the back of his head.

Third, there will always be
that square half-inch or so of unscratchable skin
between the shoulder blades, unreachable
from over the top or underneath. And fourth,

as I once heard said, don't go inventing
the acid that will eat through anything
without giving some thought
to a jar to keep it in.

★

Mice and snakes don't give me the shivers,
which I put down squarely to a decent beginning.
Upbringing, I should say, by which I mean
how me and the old man
made a good team, and never took
to stepping outside or mixing it up, aside

from the odd time when I had one word too many
for my mother, or that underwater evening
when I came home swimming
through a quart of stolen home-brewed damson wine.

So it goes. And anyway, like he says,
on the day I'm broad and bothered and bold enough
to take a swing and try and knock his grin off,

he'll be too old.

★

I live in fear of letting people down.
Last winter, someone leaked the blueprint for a plan
to put the town back on the map:
that everyone should stand and strike a match
at midnight on the shortest, darkest day,
then photograph it from an aeroplane. No way:

the workers wouldn't break bread with the upper class,
the wealthy wouldn't mingle with the mob,
the worthy knew a thing or two about sulphuric gas.

It came to pass that only one man struck; a man whose job
or game was civic unrest and civil dissent, but who claimed
to be lighting his pipe in any event,
a man whose face turned purple as he spoke.

I know very well that man doesn't smoke.

★

I'm dreaming of that work, *Man Seated Reading*
at a Table in a Lofty Room, and while I sleep
a virus sweeps the earth, and when I wake I see
the population of the world is

me.

I take the observation suite in Emley Moor Mast
to watch the skyline from the Appalachians to the Alps;
those signs of life, a thousand miles away perhaps,
are nothing more than fireflies nesting in the grass
across the fell.

I manage very well, become a master in the arts
of food and drink and heat and light,
but then at night, with no one in the world
to cut my throat, I lock and latch
and bar and bolt the windows and the hatch.

★

Brung up with swine, I was,
and dogs,
and raised on a diet of slime and slops
and pobs, then fell in one day
with a different kind. Some say

that gives me the right
to try out that line
about having a bark and having a bite,
and a nose for uncovering truffles, or shite.
Or, put another way,

what looks from afar
like a cloak of fur
is a coat of hair. Cut back the hair to find
not skin, but rind.

★

Those bastards in their mansions:
to hear them shriek, you'd think
I'd poisoned the dogs and vaulted the ditches,
crossed the lawns in stocking feet and threadbare britches,
forced the door of one of the porches, and lifted
the gift of fire from the burning torches,

then given heat and light to streets and houses,
told the people how to ditch their cuffs and shackles,
armed them with the iron from their wrists and ankles.

Those lords and ladies in their palaces and castles,
they'd have me sniffed out by their beagles,
picked at by their eagles, pinned down, grilled
beneath the sun.

Me, I stick to the shadows, carry a gun.

★

There are those who manage their private affairs
and those who have to make a hash of theirs.

In terms of a friend of a friend of mine,
there's that rush of clean air
like bailing out five miles above the earth,
he reckons, falling free, so many feet
per second per second, hoping to land in the lap
of the world, cushioned by water, broken by ferns,
but nettled with bruises or blisters or burns,
or taken by trees, hung by the neck.

Things he should want: safety first,
a perfect match, a straight indivisible two –
he wouldn't dream of leaping.
But he don't. So he do.

★

æŋkɪˈləʊzɪŋ spɒndɪˈlaɪtɪs:
ankylosing meaning bond or join,
and spondylitis meaning of the bone or spine.
That half explains the cracks and clicks,
the clockwork of my joints and discs,
the ratchet of my hips. I'm fossilizing –
every time I rest
I let the gristle knit, weave, mesh.

My dear, my skeleton will set like biscuit overnight,
like glass, like ice, and you can choose
to snap me back to life before first light,
or let me laze until
the shape I take becomes the shape I keep.

Don't leave me be. Don't let me sleep.

★

Let this matchstick be a brief biography,
the sign or symbol
for the lifetime of a certain someone.

How a spark of light
went to his head, but
how that halo soon came loose,
became a noose,
a girdle, then a belt, a Hula-Hoop
of inflammation spreading through his frame
to take his legs and black his boots,

and left him spent, bent
out of line,
a saint, burnt at the stake,
the spine.

★

I've made out a will; I'm leaving myself
to the National Health. I'm sure they can use
the jellies and tubes and syrups and glues,
the web of nerves and veins, the loaf of brains,
an assortment of fillings and stitches and wounds,
blood – a gallon exactly of bilberry soup –
the chassis or cage or cathedral of bone;
but not the heart, they can leave that alone.

They can have the lot, the whole stock:
the loops and coils and sprockets and springs and rods,
the twines and cords and strands,
the face, the case, the cogs and the hands,

but not the pendulum, the ticker;
leave that where it stops or hangs.

★

I thought I'd write my own obituary. Instead,
I wrote the blurb for when I'm risen from the dead:

Ignite the flares, connect the phones, wind all the clocks;
the sun goes rusty like a medal in its box –
collect it from the loft. Peg out the stars,
replace the bulbs of Jupiter and Mars.
A man like that takes something with him when he dies,
but he has wept the coins that rested on his eyes,
eased out the stopper from the mouthpiece of the cave,
exhumed his own white body from the grave.

Unlock the rivers, hoist the dawn and launch the sea.
Set up the skittles of the orchard and the wood again,
now everything is clear and straight and free and good
again.

★

Life:
behind the spreading butter comes the knife;
the deaf and dumb and blind man dozing
in a field of rape, found by the sickle
or the scythe. I'd been supposing

that it all adds up
to something times the power
of infinity recurring, but

it doesn't take a flying pass
in Further Maths
to figure out the sum
of what's already gone, what's going on
and what's to come.
It's none.

★

I have dreams like nightmares where I am deserted
and alone. So once again we round the final bend
of Waters Road, and up ahead the headlights project
a single subject in a silver picture.
You walk out into the scene, and lift her.

Dead weight in your hands, you hold the kitten
like the proof of something: the mouth and nose
in the wrong plane, the eyes unbuttoned from their holes,
the lips undone, the slip of the tongue ... With a spade
I carve a space in the garden, the blackness;
you fold her in, I stroke the soft earth back across.

All night, beside ourselves, we will not touch, and flinch
from any thought or word of what was done,
as if burnt by the sun.

★

I think about the time
we find we hold the loose end of the family line.

The milk and the post arrive with a baby.
The arm of the chair is nursing a cushion, a baby.
The windows are daubed with the sign of a baby. Outside,
a dog runs off with the name of a baby.

You bake a cake but cradle the bowl. From the garden
I come with potatoes, tomatoes, empty-handed.
The sound of a clock as it stops is shocking. Shocking.
The cat gets deep down in a basket of washing.

Walk with me out of town, wearing my coat,
under my arm, without the fat face of the moon
to stamp against the stone
the shadow of ourselves, and ourselves only.

★

I feel I am at the end of my tether
and don't want to go on any longer.
Not like those climbers on Malham Cove –
dipping backwards for their bags of powder,
reaching upwards for the next hairline fracture,
hauling themselves from my binoculars.

And without enlargement they take on the scale
of last night's stars in Malham Tarn,
inching upstream as the universe tilted, mirrored
till we burst their colours with a fistful of cinders.

I follow a line
from the base to the summit, waiting
for something to give, to lose its footing,
for signs of life on other planets.

★

No convictions – that's my one major fault.
Nothing to tempt me to scream and shout, nothing
to raise Cain or make a song and dance about.

A man like me could be a real handful,
steeping himself overnight in petrol,
becoming inflamed on behalf of the world,
letting his blood boil, letting his hair curl.

I have a beauty spot three inches south-east
of my nose, a heart that has to be a match
for any pocket watch, a fist
that opens like a fine Swiss Army knife,
and certain tricks that have been known
to bring about spontaneous applause.
But no cause, no cause.

★

The story changes every time.
That shadow on my back, behind my heart, has been
a blemish and a birthmark and a burn,
but in the mirror looks like something else to me.
It's you, my twin,
it's where they slit the skin that fused us,
where they pruned us, where they cut me free.

The others couple off, split up,
forget the roots, but me

I hack off to the library, find you there
on microfiche, about my age,
about my build, about my height.
I was right:

suicide.

★

Thinking back, they either pulled me like a tooth,
or drew me like a rabbit from a hat,
or else I came to life
like something frantic from under the ice

on Sunday the twenty-sixth of May
nineteen sixty-three.
It was thirteen hundred hours, GMT.

Whichever way, it's either passed me by
at something close to the speed of light,
or else I've lived it frame by frame, the whole
slow-motion picture show,
as if that day were thirty years, nine hours,
eleven minutes, five,
six, seven spasms of the second hand ago.

★

Some unimportant word or phrase
runs through my mind, on and off, for days.
Light the blue touch and stand well back.
Never return to a smouldering jumping jack.

Tonight I'm blank, burnt out, parked
in the garage, with the engine running, in the dark.
The ones who know me hold me at arm's length,
the others want to see me dead.

Not yet.
I tear the last match from the book,
fetch it hard and once
across the windscreen. In the glass

I'm taken with myself, caught in the act –
conducting light, until the heat licks
up against my thumb and fingertips, unlocks
my hand, gives me a start, trips

something in the flashbulb of my heart.

II — BECOMING OF AGE

Map Reference

Not that it was the first peak in the range,
or the furthest.
It didn't have the swankiest name
and wasn't the highest even, or the finest.

In fact, if those in the know
ever had their say about sea-level or cross-sections,
or had their way with angles and vectors,
or went there with their instruments about them,
it might have been more of a hill than a mountain.

As for its features,
walls fell into stones along its lower reaches,
fields ran up against its footslopes, scree had loosened
from around its shoulders. Incidentally, pine trees
pitched about its south and west approaches.

We could have guessed, I think, had we taken to it,
the view, straightforward, from its summit.

So,
as we rounded on it from the road that day,
how very smart of me to say or not to say
what we both knew:
that it stood where it stood, so absolutely, for you.

The Lost Letter of the Late Jud Fry

Wake.
And in my head
walk barefoot, naked from the bed
towards the day, then
wait.

Hold.
The dawn will crack
its egg into the morning's bowl
and him on horseback,
gold.

Me,
I'm in the shed, I'm
working on it: a plus b plus c, it's
you, him, me. It's
three.

Hell,
this hole, this shack.
The sun makes light of me
behind my back.
Well,

good.
I give you the applause
of ringdoves lifting from the wood
and, for an encore,
blood.

Look,
see, no man
should be me, the very opposite
of snowman:
soot.

I
work that black dust
where I slice your name into my forearm
with a jackknife: L.A.U.R.E.
Y.

You
at the window now,
undressed. I underestimated him,
never saw you as a pair, a
two.

Yours –
that's him for sure.
The sun will have its day,
its weeks, months,
years.

Fine.
But just for once, for me,
dig deep, think twice, be otherwise, be
someone else this time.
Mine.

To Poverty
after Laycock

You are near again, and have been there
or thereabouts for years. Pull up a chair.
I'd know that shadow anywhere, that silhouette
without a face, that shape. Well, be my guest.
We'll live like sidekicks – hip to hip,
like Siamese twins, joined at the pocket.

I've tried too long to see the back of you.
Last winter when you came down with the flu
I should have split, cut loose, but
let you pass the buck, the bug. Bad blood.
It's cold again; come closer to the fire, the light,
and let me make you out.

How have you hurt me, let me count the ways:
the months of Sundays
when you left me in the damp, the dark,
the red, or down and out, or out of work.
The weeks on end of bread without butter,
bed without supper.

That time I fell through Schofield's shed
and broke both legs,
and Schofield couldn't spare to split
one stick of furniture to make a splint.
Thirteen weeks I sat there till they set.
What can the poor do but wait? And wait.

How come you're struck with me? Go see the Queen,
lean on the doctor or the dean,
breathe on the major,
squeeze the mason or the manager,
go down to London, find a novelist at least
to bother with, to bleed, to leech.

On second thoughts, stay put.
A person needs to get a person close enough
to stab him in the back.
Robert Frost said that. Besides,
I'd rather keep you in the corner of my eye
than wait for you to join me side by side
at every turn, on every street, in every town.
Sit down. I said sit down.

Tale

It's told like this:
the five of them, up with the lark
to get to Leeds, to change, like
five small dogs out for the first time off

the lead. They were drinking beer.
They were all fourteen.
That train, those carriages, compartments,
self-contained without a corridor or toilet,

anywhere to let off steam
or take a leak. Except, with one foot
on each seat, and with his head
above the luggage-rack, out of the window

one amongst them passed
a golden, exponential curve of piss.
This being a through train not a stopping one
made it a narrow miss for anyone

on Preston Station, mistaken,
moving forward to make a connection.
Further down the line the image is
five little angels

lying through their teeth
to a serious man from the Railway Police.
Eye-witnesses insist on looking for a likeness.
Identity parade is what the bottom line is.

Reverse Charge

Long distance – would I accept it? Wavelengths
bristled, or a spine of fibre optics
warmed to what the message was, wormed its way
across a seabed and a mountain range.
I said 'You've changed.'

Seventeen hundred miles, but every verb
delivered in the bubble of its breath,
as if we held each other by the neck,
each word as if each word had just happened.
She said 'You haven't.'

You

hold the page out like a work of art,
see for yourself, comb through it twice, three times,
look for your likeness in the lines but find
someone else.

When did I ever see you wear a hat?
You certainly never said that. Or that.
Fiction, I say. You take the page again,
catch the light,

see through it once, then twice, then strike a match.
I am a cheat, a bastard, and a liar.
You tear it into two, four, eight, sixteen,
feed the fire.

Parable of the Dead Donkey

Instructions arrived by registered post
under cover of separate envelopes:
directions first
to pinpoint the place
in the shape of maps and compass bearings;
those, then forms and stamps for loss of earnings.
So much was paid
to diggers of graves
by keepers or next of kin, peg leg
(which made for the dumping of quadrupeds):
sixteen quid
to send off a pig
or sink a pit for a dog or pony.
But less to plant a man than a donkey.
Cheaper by half
for a pregnant horse
that died with all four hooves inside her
than one with a stillborn foal beside her.
And this was a bind,
being duty bound
where ownership was unestablished.
We filled the flasks and loaded the Transit,
then set out, making
for the undertaking.

Facing north, he was dead at three o'clock
in a ring of meadow grass, closely cropped,
where a metal chain
on a wooden stake
had stopped him ambling off at an angle,

worn him down in a perfect circle.
We burrowed in
right next to him
through firm white soil. An hour's hard labour
took us five feet down – and then the weather:
thunder biting
the heels of lightning,
a cloudburst drawing a curtain of rain
across us, filling the bath of the grave,
and we waded in it
for one more minute,
dredged and shovelled as the tide was rising,
bailed out for fear of drowning, capsizing.
Back on top
we weighed him up,
gave some thought to this beast of the Bible:
the nose and muzzle, the teeth, the eyeballs,
the rump, the hindquarters,
the flanks, the shoulders,
everything soothed in the oil of the rain –
the eel of his tongue, the keel of his spine,
the rope of his tail,
the weeds of his mane.
Then we turned him about and slipped his anchor,
eased him out of the noose of his tether,
and rolled him in
and started to dig.
But even with donkey, water and soil
there wasn't enough to level the hole
after what was washed away
or turned into clay
or trodden in, so we opened the earth
and started in on a second trench for dirt

to fill the first.
Which left a taste
of starting something that wouldn't finish:
a covered grave with a donkey in it,
a donkey-size hole
within a stone's throw
and not a single bone to drop in it
or a handful of dust to toss on top of it.

The van wouldn't start, so we wandered home
on foot, in the dark, without supper or profit.

Hitcher

I'd been tired, under
the weather, but the ansaphone kept screaming:
One more sick-note, mister, and you're finished. Fired.
I thumbed a lift to where the car was parked.
A Vauxhall Astra. It was hired.

I picked him up in Leeds.
He was following the sun to west from east
with just a toothbrush and the good earth for a bed. The truth,
he said, was blowin' in the wind,
or round the next bend.

I let him have it
on the top road out of Harrogate – once
with the head, then six times with the krooklok
in the face – and didn't even swerve.
I dropped it into third

and leant across
to let him out, and saw him in the mirror
bouncing off the kerb, then disappearing down the verge.
We were the same age, give or take a week.
He'd said he liked the breeze

to run its fingers
through his hair. It was twelve noon.
The outlook for the day was moderate to fair.
Stitch that, I remember thinking,
you can walk from there.

Act of Union

Go on, go down beneath the sheet.
I think I have a secret you can keep.
Below the skin it's dark. Not clear. Not clean.
This is my blood, my body, and my seed.
Eat. Drink. Do this in remembrance of me.

Cataract Operation

The sun comes like a head
through last night's turtleneck.

A pigeon in the yard turns tail
and offers me a card. Any card.

From pillar to post, a pantomime
of damp, forgotten washing

on the washing line.
So, in the breeze:

the olé of a crimson towel,
the cancan of a ra ra skirt,

the monkey business of a shirt
pegged only by its sleeve,

the cheerio
of a handkerchief.

I drop the blind
but not before a company

of half a dozen hens
struts through the gate,

looks round the courtyard
for a contact lens.

On the Trail of the Old Ways

Start from a heath, which is the true heart
of a house.
Face south. Walk forward to the nearest mound.
Go east alone
through castle, crossroads, smithy, hallowed ground;
pass on the right
a standing stone. Pick up a tooth, a feather
or a bone.
Next, take a bearing to the Long or Lone
or Lanky Man,
take in a well, a church, a single birch,
make for a copse,
go three times round a moat. Unearth a flint
or coin,
then find a ditch or pond to let it sink
or make it skim.
The gate between two trees leads to a road;
walk north,
then west towards the sun to where it sets.
Look left
and ford the brook. There they are. Pick them up.

Penelope

your man is long gone, and I have loitered
by your garden gate; weeded the border,
turned the soil over, waited on your word.

There is a quilt or sheet or counterpane
strung out across a tenterframe; by day
you make it, sitting in the window seat.

And you have crossed your heart and hoped
to die, promised that this cover, blanket,
bedspread, when completed, will envelop me
with you.
           Penelope, one night last June
I came for fruit, and from the crow's nest
of the cherry tree I made you out:
unhitching one day's stitching, teasing knot
from thread, releasing warp from weft ...
I dropped down from the tree and left.

That's fine. You're buying time, holding your breath,
watching, waiting for your man to show.

I'm in the garden picking you a rose:
this new strain with their frantic, crimson heads,
open now and at their very best, having dozed
all winter in a deep, rich bed, the trench
I sank one evening by the potting shed.
I mark the best bloom, take it at the neck.

To His Lost Lover

Now they are no longer
any trouble to each other

he can turn things over, get down to that list
of things that never happened, all of the lost

unfinishable business.
For instance ... for instance,

how he never clipped and kept her hair, or drew a hairbrush
through that style of hers, and never knew how not to blush

at the fall of her name in close company.
How they never slept like buried cutlery –

two spoons or forks cupped perfectly together,
or made the most of some heavy weather –

walked out into hard rain under sheet lightning,
or did the gears while the other was driving.

How he never raised his fingertips
to stop the segments of her lips

from breaking the news,
or tasted the fruit,

or picked for himself the pear of her heart,
or lifted her hand to where his own heart

was a small, dark, terrified bird
in her grip. Where it hurt.

Or said the right thing,
or put it in writing.

And never fled the black mile back to his house
before midnight, or coaxed another button of her blouse,

then another,
or knew her

favourite colour,
her taste, her flavour,

and never ran a bath or held a towel for her,
or soft-soaped her, or whipped her hair

into an ice-cream cornet or a beehive
of lather, or acted out of turn, or misbehaved

when he might have, or worked a comb
where no comb had been, or walked back home

through a black mile hugging a punctured heart,
where it hurt, where it hurt, or helped her hand

to his butterfly heart
in its two blue halves.

And never almost cried,
and never once described

an attack of the heart,
or under a silk shirt

nursed in his hand her breast,
her left, like a tear of flesh

wept by the heart,
where it hurts,

or brushed with his thumb the nut of her nipple,
or drank intoxicating liquors from her navel.

Or christened the Pole Star in her name,
or shielded the mask of her face like a flame,

a pilot light,
or stayed the night,

or steered her back to that house of his,
or said 'Don't ask me to say how it is

I like you.
I just might do.'

How he never figured out a fireproof plan,
or unravelled her hand, as if her hand

were a solid ball
of silver foil

and discovered a lifeline hiding inside it,
and measured the trace of his own alongside it.

But said some things and never meant them –
sweet nothings anybody could have mentioned.

And left unsaid some things he should have spoken,
about the heart, where it hurt exactly, and how often.

Becoming of Age

The year the institutions would not hold.
The autumn when the convicts took their leave.
The month the radio went haywire, gargled
through the long-range forecast, and their names.
The fortnight of the curfew, and the cheese-wire
of the Klaxon slicing day from night, night
from day. The clear, unclouded ocean

of the sky. The week we met. The afternoon
we might have seen a ghost, a scarecrow
striding boldly down The Great North Road
towards us, wearing everything he owned.

The minute in the phone box with the coin,
the dialling tone, the disagreement – heads
to turn him in to the authorities, or tails
to leave him be, to let him go to ground
and keep the public footpaths trodden down,
the green lanes and the bridleways.

Then on the glass, each in its own time – one,
two, three, four, five, six fingerprints of rain.

III — READING THE BANNS

Above me, at the abbey,
from the window

where you wonder ... if
you let your golden hair

unfurl from there, a lifeline, curl
by curl, unload it

down the wall ...
I will. I will.

At closer inspection,
those waves of ink

across the writing pad
are not a child's interpretation

of the ocean, or the notion
of a line from here to there

for no apparent reason
concertinaed, or the shorthand

for a troupe of seagulls
hanging wing to wing

across the middle distance
of a picture,

but the first attempts
at your new signature.

Tread carefully:
the issue of the guest list

and the menu
has more corns than toes.

Who stops, who goes,
who stays at home,

who shall have roast beef,
who shall have none.

This time the cat
has gone too far; she sidles back

across the lazy river
with a kingfisher.

You pin her to the floor, unlock
the trap of her jaw,

release the teeth,
unpick the four barbed feet, each paw

a presentation pad of claws.
The bird can walk;

you let it go, but in the morning
find it cornered, killed, and opened.

Something blue, something bone,
something gold, something broken.

A dream, a nightmare:
in the church

an hour before the service, unaccompanied,
the congregation practising

their just impediments, in unison.
And then the photograph:

your mother and mine
in identical hats, arm in arm

along the aisle
into the flash.

Snap.

This 1950 Rolls-Royce Silver Wraith
is twenty quid

above the going rate
but twice as stately as the Bentley

or the green Mecedes-Benz.
We'll take it.

In its double berth
we test the leather,

see ourselves together
in the rear-view mirror,

draw the blind
that separates the back seat

from the driver and his line of sight.
We can't wait.

With her labrador, at night,
a Cyclops in a caving hat

or Davy lamp, your mother
out along the lane

for exercise, for air,
until her one bright eye

rounds on a dozen magpies
in the popeye tree.

A dozen magpies in the popeye tree?
What does that mean?

Around the cuffs and neck at least
two thousand pearls or beads

to fix by hand.
Each line is threaded, double tied –

one broken link will turn the church
into a roller-skating rink.

And anyway, the dress is not for me
to see; you have it covered

in a second skin, a bag, and reach inside
to go on patiently transplanting

from the never-ending jar
of pearls or beads.

You could be peeling prawns,
or shelling peas.

Nine morning suits:
five ushers,

fathers on each side,
a best man and a groom.

Nine morning suits
all hanging from the picture rail,

all covered, zipped, and tagged.
Nine body bags.

At this stage in the day,
no one wants to risk a graze

or tennis elbow.
No one wants to twist an ankle,

black an eye or break a nail.
So at three games all

in the final set
your lunge for the ball

is a half-hearted trawl
with a fishing net,

and my second service
not much better

than the hopeful scoop
of a butterfly collector.

Your wedding day requires
a suntan greater than the year provides.

For forty minutes at a time
the sunbed with its eight fluorescent tubes

ticks over in the other room, with you
in goggles and a level teaspoonful of oil

becoming blasé, brazen,
turning occasionally,

burning eventually.
Outside, the evening deepens

and the light escaping
from between the curtains

brightens out of lilac
into ultraviolet.

Let me put it this way:
if you came to lay

your sleeping head
against my arm or sleeve,

and if my arm went dead,
or if I had to take my leave

at midnight, I should rather
cleave it from the joint or seam

than make a scene
or bring you round.

There,
how does that sound?